Memories of You

Pet Memory Book

This pet memory book is dedicated to:

_____

(Your pet's name)

My Pet Memory Book

Pets are very special friends. They stick by us through thick and thin. Even when we have bad days, our pets show us love and comfort. When we are happy, they are always ready to play. Some pets even get to sleep in our beds with us.

Losing a pet makes us very, very sad.

This memory book is designed to help you create memories about your pet that you can keep to remember the wonderful times you had together.

Draw a picture of your pet.

My pet was a _____

My pet's name was _____

The thing I loved most about my pet

_____

_____

_____

The thing I miss most about my pet is

_____

_____

_____

When did you get your pet? _____

Where did you get your pet? _____

Draw a picture of the first day you got your pet.
If you have one you'd like to paste or tape instead,
you can do that.

How did you feel when you first met your pet?

_____

_____

What is something you did for your new pet?

_____

_____

People have a lot of feelings about raising a pet.
Circle the feelings you had below.
If some of your feelings are not mentioned, add them on the lines below.

Happy	Excited	Nervous	Intrigued
Proud	Encouraged	Compassionate	Grateful
Energetic	Tender	Delighted	Hopeful

_____   _____   _____

There are also a lot of feelings that come with losing a beloved pet.
Circle the feelings you had below.
If some of your feelings are not mentioned, add them on the lines below.

Angry	Sad	Lonely	Afraid
Disbelief	Discouraged	Sympathetic	Confused
Worried	Anxious	Guilty	Lost
		Relieved	

_____   _____   _____

Some of these feelings might have been brand new to you.
If you hadn't felt these feelings before you raised and lost your pet, circle
them again in a different color.

In the mirror, draw a picture of how you felt when your pet passed away.

Exercise

When you are angry, exercise can make you feel a lot better. You may walk around your neighborhood, ride your bike, or take ballet lessons. What are the different ways you enjoy exercising? Name your favorite kinds of exercise below, then pick the one you like best and draw a picture of your self doing that activity.

Name the exercise you are performing in the picture: _____

How does this exercise make you feel? _____

Are you less angry after you exercise? Have you tried performing this exercise when you were angry?

Thoughts

Thoughts are important because they tell us things about our world and how we feel about it. Some thoughts get stuck in our head, like a song we hear on the radio over and over. But you get to control your thoughts! Thoughts are what we tell ourselves. You might think, "I miss my pet and I am sad."

Feelings

Feelings are what we experience in our emotions and bodies. They can be happy, sad, nervous, or something else; there are many feelings. All feelings are good, though we prefer some feelings to others.

Draw a picture of you and your pet doing something that makes you feel happy.

Actions

Actions are what we do—usually with our bodies.
We choose our actions, such as playing with our pets.
Draw a picture of yourself playing wiht your pet.

Sometimes, when someone goes away, we want to perform an action to show how we feel and how much we miss them. There are many things we can do to show our pets we love them after they die.

Here's something you can do:

Ask your loved one to buy you a helium-filled balloon. Write a message on it to your pet with a marker (be careful not to pop the balloon). Then go outside, let the balloon go, and imagine your pet getting your balloon message when it's floating high in the sky.

If you wrote a balloon message to your pet, what would it say? Write your message below to practice before buying your real balloon.

_____

_____

_____

_____

_____

_____

_____

Crying is okay—it's a way to release our sadness. Tears are a healthy way to express when we're sad. You may have cried a lot when your pet died.

Can you draw a picture of a tear below, and then explain how you feel after you cry? Are you relieved, tired, or still sad but you feel a little better?

When I cry, I feel

_____

When I am done crying, I feel

_____

Pet
Page Memories

Read the poem below, then illustrate it with a drawing of you and your pet on the next page.

My Best Friend

My pet and I were the very best of friends.

We played, made trouble, and then made amends.

Every day I fed my pet

With food approved by our favorite vet.

I shared my secrets and my pet listened close.

I think that is what I will miss the most.

But for now, my pet has died and gone away.

And I must go on, living happy every day.

That will not be easy at first, I know,

But I will remember our good times and keep them in tow.

There are days that I feel very sad

But I know that my memories will help me get glad.

My Pet and Me

Your pet was special for many reasons. In the ribbon below, award your pet the honor of best friend prize. Then color the ribbon.

What do you think your pet was the best at doing? What made your pet special? Draw or write your thoughts in the bubbles below.

Each pet is special in its own way. Finish the sentences below, then draw a picture of each description inside the frames. This way, you will always remember the special details about your pet.

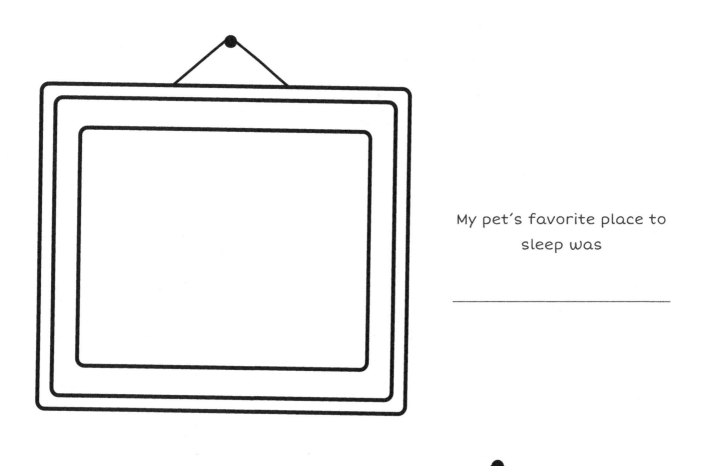

My pet's favorite place to sleep was

_____

My pet's favorite snack food was

_____

Every day, my pet would

_____

My pet's favorite game to play was

_____

What do you think your pet would've wanted you to know if he or she could've communicated with you? Write or draw the thoughts you think your pet might have had in the thought bubble below.

Sometimes, people try to help us feel better after our pet passes away by saying things they think are comforting but are not really helpful. And sometimes, the things people say are helpful. Read the statements in each speech bubble below that might have been said to you. In the thought bubbles, write or draw the feelings or thoughts you had when they were said to you.

Your thoughts might be very angry or sad. These are normal, healthy feelings to have. However, it is not okay to speak angrily to someone when you have angry feelings—especially when the person you're speaking to has good intentions and is saying what they think might help you. Sometimes it can be helpful to have a response ready to handle these difficult conversations, so try practicing by preparing one on the lines below.

"Thank you for saying that, but right now I am feeling

_____

_____

_____

_____

_____

_____

_____

_____

_____

_____

_____

_____

This page is for you to remember the day your pet passed away. There might be a lot of confusion about this day, because some of the feelings you had might have changed since then.

The day I learned my pet passed away was on	My pet passed away at
_____ told me that my pet had died/was going to die.	When I first heard the news, I felt

This is a picture of the day I learned my pet passed away:

The day I lost my pet was very sad. That day, I felt sadder than I'd ever felt before. Today, I feel _____. Some days are harder than others, and thats okay. I know I will be okay. Still, I know it is okay to cry when I need to. I know I can talk about my feelings—happy or sad. My feelings matter. My feelings are what make me ME.

Have you ever heard the phrase, "Rain makes the flowers grow."? Sometimes the rain can represent sad times, while the flowers represent happy times that come along after. Write some of your sad feelings in the rain clouds below, and some of your happy feelings in the flowers.

Always remember that good times follow bad times, no matter how bad they get.

Did you know it is normal for kids who lose a pet to feel guilty? Sometimes they feel like it is their fault their pet got sick, injured, or even old and died. It helps to remember the wonderful, helpful things we did for our pets, and the reasons they loved us so much. In the hearts on the left side below, write or draw something you did for your pet to show love. On the right, write or draw something your pet did to show you love.

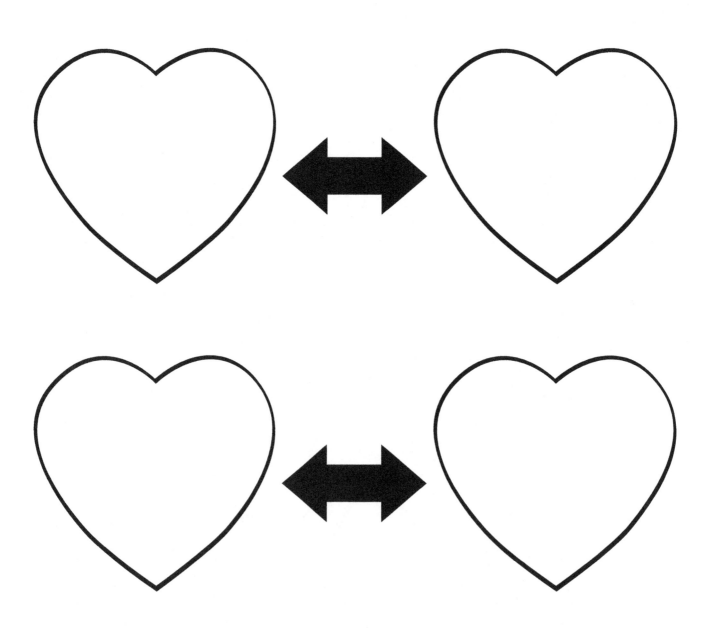

Setting Aside Some Special Time

Sometimes, it is helpful to deal with the sad feelings you have after losing a pet to hold a special service to remember him or her—kind of like a funeral or memorial service. You may not be able to actually bury your pet (or maybe you can), but you can still designate a special place and time to remember him or her. You might want to pick a spot in the backyard, or keep a picture inside your home as your remembering place. For your special service, you could invite your friends over, or just stick with your family, to spend time remembering your pet together. It is ok to cry at your special service. Many people cry and laugh at memorial services. These special times are set aside to focus on feelings. Happiness and sadness are expressed so people can start to feel better.

Today, or whenever you feel ready, talk to your family about having a service for your pet if you have not had one yet. Even if your pet passed away a while ago, you might want to remember it with a service. You can also remember the anniversary of your service each year, if you choose.

Part of big, bad feelings can come from being confused. When we don't understand something, we can become even more scared, sad, or even mad. Losing a pet can make you think of a lot of questions. These can be confusing, and you might be scared to ask them. Write any quesitons you might have inside each questions mark below. Do you think that you would feel better if your questions were answered? Go ahead and try asking them and see if you do. Start with choosing one question, and ask a trusted adult if he or she can talk about it with you.

Sometimes it can be very hard to deal with bad feelings. They can feel very big—bigger than we think we can handle. In the box below, write the bad feelings you have that feel very big. Write them as big as they feel. Then cut out the box (have an adult help) and fold it as small as you want your feelings to feel. When you are ready, you can even throw the paper away.

Another feeling that goes along with losing a pet is feeling like you are powerless. One way to deal with this feeling is to make wishes. They might not come true in the way that we wish them, but they do give us hope and something positive to focus on while we wait. Write or draw your wishes in the stars below.

Writing a letter to our lost loved ones helps us feel better. Write a letter to your pet, describing the things you miss most.

Dear _____

_____

_____

_____

_____

_____

_____

_____

_____

_____

_____

Love Always,

_____

On the board below, keep track of how you feel each day. Choose a color for each feeling, then color a square per day next to each to show what you are feeling that day. You can write in your own feelings, or choose from those in the box by circling them with the color of your choice.

Sad

Hopeful

Happy

Powerless

Powerful

Angry

Afraid

Peaceful

Fearless

Guilty

Best Friends

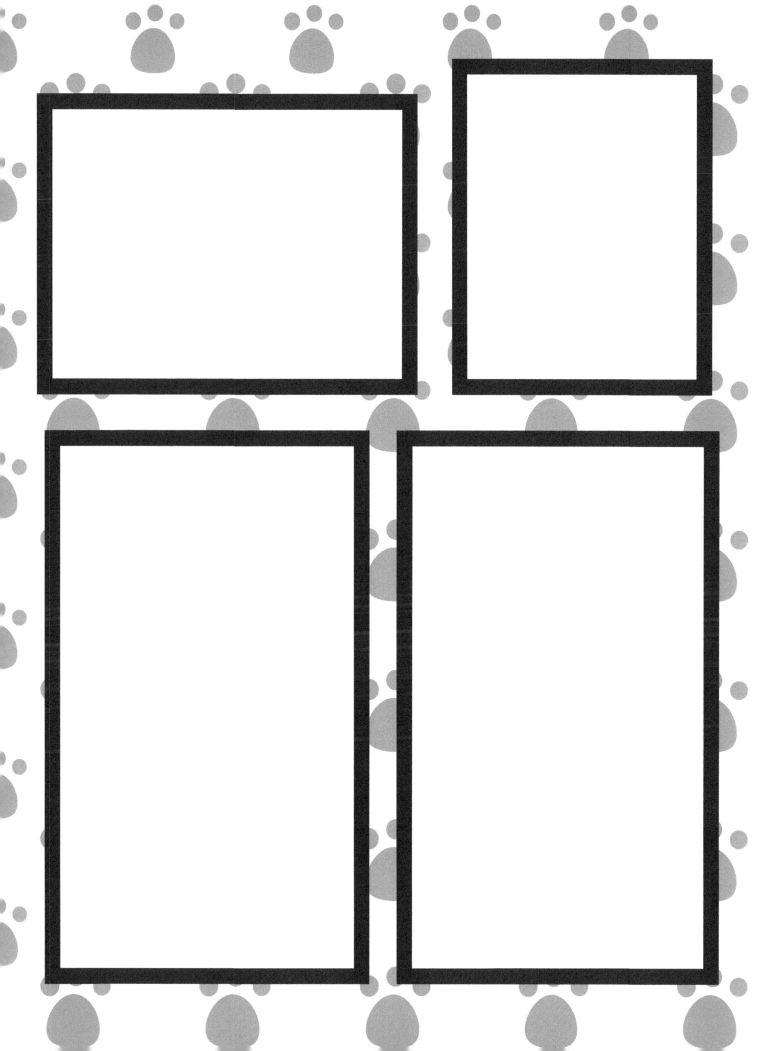

LIVE

🐾 🐾 🐾

LOVE

🐾 🐾 🐾

PLAY ❤️

Now that you have completed your memory book, keep it to remember the happy times with your pet.

color me
HAPPY

HOW TO USE THIS REFLECTION JOURNAL

Now that you've completed the activities in this workbook, it's time to focus on putting everything you learned into practice.

What does that mean? It means using the things you've learned to help you each day.

Make a plan for each morning; then at the end of the day, before bedtime, think about your day.

What was good about it?
What brought you joy?
What went wrong?
How did you handle it?
What can you do to have a great day tomorrow?

HOW TO USE THIS REFLECTION JOURNAL

STEP 1: Each morning make a plan for your day by completing side 1 of that day's journal page.

STEP 2: Each evening complete side 2 as you reflect on your day.

DATE: S M T W TH F S ___/___/___

ONLY POSITIVE THOUGHTS IN MY DAY
I can make today awesome by:

_____

_____

_____

DRAW IT!

what are you looking forward to most today?

I LOVE MYSELF
LIST 3 THINGS YOU LOVE ABOUT YOURSELF

WHAT IS SOMETHING THAT MAKES YOU HAPPY

_____

_____

_____

TODAY I FELT

SOMETHING GREAT THAT HAPPENED TODAY

_____

_____

_____

 THIS PERSON BROUGHT ME JOY TODAY

_____

_____

DATE: S M T W TH F S ___/___/___

ONLY POSITIVE THOUGHTS IN MY DAY

I can make today awesome by:

_____

_____

_____

DRAW IT!

what are you looking forward to most today?

I LOVE MYSELF

LIST 3 words that describe you

WHAT DO YOU LIKE TO DO FOR FUN

_____

_____

_____

TODAY I FELT

SOMETHING GREAT THAT HAPPENED TODAY

_____

_____

_____

THIS PERSON BROUGHT ME JOY TODAY

_____

_____

DATE: S M T W TH F S ___/___/___

ONLY POSITIVE THOUGHTS IN MY DAY
I can make today awesome by:

_____

_____

_____

DRAW IT!

what are you
looking forward
to most today?

I LOVE MYSELF
LIST 3 THINGS you are really good at doing

WHAT IS ONE OF YOUR FAVORITE MEMORIES

_____

_____

_____

TODAY I FELT

SOMETHING GREAT THAT HAPPENED TODAY

_____

_____

_____

 THIS PERSON BROUGHT ME JOY TODAY

_____

_____

DATE: S M T W TH F S ___/___/___

ONLY POSITIVE THOUGHTS IN MY DAY
I can make today awesome by:

_____

_____

_____

DRAW IT!

what are you
looking forward
to most today?

I LOVE MYSELF
LIST 3 THINGS YOU LOVE DOING

WHO IS A PERSON YOU ADMIRE (LIKE)

_____

_____

_____

TODAY I FELT

SOMETHING GREAT THAT HAPPENED TODAY

_____

_____

_____

THIS PERSON BROUGHT ME JOY TODAY

_____

_____

DATE: S M T W TH F S   ___/___/___

ONLY POSITIVE THOUGHTS IN MY DAY
I can make today awesome by:

_____

_____

_____

DRAW IT!

what are you looking forward to most today?

I LOVE MYSELF
LIST 3 THINGS YOU'D LIKE TO improve about yourself

WHAT IS SOMETHING THAT MAKES YOU PROUD?

_____

_____

_____

TODAY I FELT

SOMETHING GREAT THAT HAPPENED TODAY

_____

_____

_____

THIS PERSON BROUGHT ME JOY TODAY

_____

_____

DATE: S M T W TH F S ___/___/___

ONLY POSITIVE THOUGHTS IN MY DAY
I can make today awesome by:

_____

_____

_____

DRAW IT!

what are you
looking forward
to most today?

I LOVE MYSELF
LIST 3 THINGS THAT BRING YOU HAPPINESS

WHO IS THE KINDEST PERSON YOU KNOW

_____

_____

_____

TODAY I FELT

SOMETHING GREAT THAT HAPPENED TODAY

_____

_____

_____

THIS PERSON BROUGHT ME JOY TODAY

_____

_____

DATE: S M T W TH F S ___/___/___

ONLY POSITIVE THOUGHTS IN MY DAY
I can make today awesome by:

_____

_____

_____

DRAW IT!

what are you
looking forward
to most today?

I LOVE MYSELF
WRITE 3 WORDS TO DESCRIBE YOUR LIFE

DID I TRY SOMETHING NEW TODAY?

_____

_____

_____

TODAY I FELT

SOMETHING GREAT THAT HAPPENED TODAY

_____

_____

_____

THIS PERSON BROUGHT ME JOY TODAY

_____

_____

DATE: S M T W TH F S ___/___/___

ONLY POSITIVE THOUGHTS IN MY DAY
I can make today awesome by:

_____

_____

_____

DRAW IT!

what are you
looking forward
to most today?

I LOVE MYSELF
LIST 3 THINGS WORDS TO DESCRIBE YOUR FAMILY

DID I GET OUT OF MY COMFORT ZONE TODAY?

_____

_____

_____

TODAY I FELT

SOMETHING GREAT THAT HAPPENED TODAY

_____

_____

_____

 ## THIS PERSON BROUGHT ME JOY TODAY

_____

_____

DATE: S M T W TH F S ___/___/___

ONLY POSITIVE THOUGHTS IN MY DAY
I can make today awesome by:

_____

_____

_____

DRAW IT!

what are you looking forward to most today?

I LOVE MYSELF
LIST 3 THINGS YOU LOVE ABOUT YOURSELF

THIS IS WHAT I COULD HAVE DONE BETTER TODAY

_____

_____

_____

TODAY I FELT

SOMETHING GREAT THAT HAPPENED TODAY

_____

_____

_____

 THIS PERSON BROUGHT ME JOY TODAY

_____

_____

DATE: S M T W TH F S ___/___/___

ONLY POSITIVE THOUGHTS IN MY DAY
I can make today awesome by:

_____

_____

_____

DRAW IT!

what are you
looking forward
to most today?

I LOVE MYSELF
LIST 3 THINGS THAT MAKE YOU SMILE

TODAY I LEARNED THIS ABOUT MYSELF

_____

_____

_____

TODAY I FELT

SOMETHING GREAT THAT HAPPENED TODAY

_____

_____

_____

 ## THIS PERSON BROUGHT ME JOY TODAY

_____

_____

DATE: S M T W TH F S ___/___/___

ONLY POSITIVE THOUGHTS IN MY DAY
I can make today awesome by:

_____

_____

_____

DRAW IT!

what are you
looking forward
to most today?

I LOVE MYSELF
WRITE 3 THINGS THAT ARE GREAT ABOUT YOU

WHAT I'M LOVING ABOUT LIFE RIGHT NOW

_____

_____

_____

TODAY I FELT

SOMETHING GREAT THAT HAPPENED TODAY

_____

_____

_____

 THIS PERSON BROUGHT ME JOY TODAY

_____

_____

DATE: S M T W TH F S ___/___/___

ONLY POSITIVE THOUGHTS IN MY DAY
I can make today awesome by:

_____

_____

_____

DRAW IT!

what are you looking forward to most today?

I LOVE MYSELF
NAME 3 PEOPLE WHO BRING YOU HAPPINESS

_____

_____

_____

TODAY I FELT

SOMETHING GREAT THAT HAPPENED TODAY

_____

_____

_____

 THIS PERSON BROUGHT ME JOY TODAY

_____

_____

DATE: S M T W TH F S ___/___/___

ONLY POSITIVE THOUGHTS IN MY DAY

I can make today awesome by:

_____

_____

_____

DRAW IT!

what are you looking forward to most today?

I LOVE MYSELF

NAME 3 THINGS YOUR FRIENDS THINK YOU ARE AWESOME AT

TOMORROW I WILL SHOW KINDNESS TO THIS PERSON

_____

_____

_____

TODAY I FELT

SOMETHING GREAT THAT HAPPENED TODAY

_____

_____

_____

THIS PERSON BROUGHT ME JOY TODAY

_____

_____

DATE: S M T W TH F S ___/___/___

ONLY POSITIVE THOUGHTS IN MY DAY
I can make today awesome by:

_____

_____

_____

DRAW IT!

what are you
looking forward
to most today?

I LOVE MYSELF
WRITE 3 THINGS YOUR CLASSMATES SAY YOU ARE GREAT AT

THIS IS WHAT I WANT TO IMPROVE ABOUT MYSELF

_____

_____

_____

TODAY I FELT

SOMETHING GREAT THAT HAPPENED TODAY

_____

_____

_____

 THIS PERSON BROUGHT ME JOY TODAY

_____

_____

DATE: S M T W TH F S ___/___/___

ONLY POSITIVE THOUGHTS IN MY DAY

I can make today awesome by:

_____

_____

_____

DRAW IT!

what are you looking forward to most today?

I LOVE MYSELF

LIST 3 THINGS YOU DO THAT MAKES YOUR FAMILY HAPPY

TODAY I.....

_____

_____

_____

TODAY I FELT

SOMETHING GREAT THAT HAPPENED TODAY

_____

_____

_____

THIS PERSON BROUGHT ME JOY TODAY

_____

_____

DATE: S M T W TH F S ___/___/___

ONLY POSITIVE THOUGHTS IN MY DAY
I can make today awesome by:

_____

_____

_____

DRAW IT!

what are you
looking forward
to most today?

I LOVE MYSELF
LIST 3 THINGS THAT MAKE YOU HAPPY

WHAT I'M LOVING ABOUT LIFE RIGHT NOW

_____

_____

_____

TODAY I FELT

SOMETHING GREAT THAT HAPPENED TODAY

_____

_____

_____

 THIS PERSON BROUGHT ME JOY TODAY

_____

_____

DATE: S M T W TH F S ___/___/___

ONLY POSITIVE THOUGHTS IN MY DAY
I can make today awesome by:

_____

_____

_____

DRAW IT!

what are you looking forward to most today?

I LOVE MYSELF
LIST 3 THINGS THAT MAKE YOU FEEL GOOD

TODAY I WANT TO.....

_____

_____

_____

TODAY I FELT

😊 🙂 😐 ☹️ 😖 😴

SOMETHING GREAT THAT HAPPENED TODAY

_____

_____

_____

THIS PERSON BROUGHT ME JOY TODAY

_____

_____

DATE: S M T W TH F S _____/_____/_____

ONLY POSITIVE THOUGHTS IN MY DAY
I can make today awesome by:

_____

_____

_____

DRAW IT!

what are you
looking forward
to most today?

I LOVE MYSELF
LIST 3 FUTURE GOALS FOR YOURSELF

TODAY'S ACTIVITIES MADE ME.....

_____

_____

_____

TODAY I FELT

SOMETHING GREAT THAT HAPPENED TODAY

_____

_____

_____

 THIS PERSON BROUGHT ME JOY TODAY

_____

_____

DATE: S M T W TH F S ___/___/___

ONLY POSITIVE THOUGHTS IN MY DAY
I can make today awesome by:

_____

_____

_____

DRAW IT!

what are you
looking forward
to most today?

I LOVE MYSELF
LIST 3 THINGS YOU ENJOY DOING

TODAY I WANTED TO....

_____

_____

_____

TODAY I FELT

😊 🙂 😐 🙁 😣 😴

SOMETHING GREAT THAT HAPPENED TODAY

_____

_____

_____

THIS PERSON BROUGHT ME JOY TODAY

_____

_____

DATE: S M T W TH F S ___/___/___

ONLY POSITIVE THOUGHTS IN MY DAY
I can make today awesome by:

_____

_____

_____

DRAW IT!

what are you looking forward to most today?

I LOVE MYSELF
LIST 3 THINGS YOU DO THAT MAKES OTHERS SMILE

IF I COULD CHANGE THIS ABOUT TODAY

_____

_____

_____

TODAY I FELT

SOMETHING GREAT THAT HAPPENED TODAY

_____

_____

_____

THIS PERSON BROUGHT ME JOY TODAY

_____

_____

DATE: S M T W TH F S ___/___/___

ONLY POSITIVE THOUGHTS IN MY DAY
I can make today awesome by:

_____

_____

_____

DRAW IT!

what are you looking forward to most today?

I LOVE MYSELF
LIST 3 THINGS YOU LOVE ABOUT YOURSELF

MY DAY WAS.....

_____

_____

_____

TODAY I FELT

SOMETHING GREAT THAT HAPPENED TODAY

_____

_____

_____

THIS PERSON BROUGHT ME JOY TODAY

_____

_____

DATE: S M T W TH F S ___/___/___

ONLY POSITIVE THOUGHTS IN MY DAY

I can make today awesome by:

_____

_____

_____

DRAW IT!

what are you looking forward to most today?

I LOVE MYSELF

WRITE 3 AFFIRMATIONS: I AM.....

I LEARNED THIS ABOUT MYSELF TODAY

_____

_____

_____

TODAY I FELT

SOMETHING GREAT THAT HAPPENED TODAY

_____

_____

_____

THIS PERSON BROUGHT ME JOY TODAY

_____

_____

DATE: S M T W TH F S ___/___/___

ONLY POSITIVE THOUGHTS IN MY DAY
I can make today awesome by:

_____

_____

_____

DRAW IT!

what are you looking forward to most today?

I LOVE MYSELF
LIST 3 GOALS YOU'D LIKE TO ACHIEVE THIS WEEK

I HOPE TOMORROW IS....

_____

_____

_____

TODAY I FELT

SOMETHING GREAT THAT HAPPENED TODAY

_____

_____

_____

THIS PERSON BROUGHT ME JOY TODAY

_____

_____

DATE: S M T W TH F S ___/___/___

ONLY POSITIVE THOUGHTS IN MY DAY

I can make today awesome by:

_____

_____

_____

DRAW IT!

what are you looking forward to most today?

I LOVE MYSELF

LIST 3 THINGS YOU HAVE ALWAYS WANTED TO DO

LIFE IS GOOD BECAUSE...

_____

_____

_____

TODAY I FELT

SOMETHING GREAT THAT HAPPENED TODAY

_____

_____

_____

 THIS PERSON BROUGHT ME JOY TODAY

_____

_____

DATE: S M T W TH F S ___/___/___

ONLY POSITIVE THOUGHTS IN MY DAY
I can make today awesome by:

_____

_____

_____

DRAW IT!
what are you looking forward to most today?

I LOVE MYSELF
LIST 3 THINGS YOU DREAM ABOUT

_____ IS MY HERO BECAUSE.....

_____

_____

_____

TODAY I FELT

SOMETHING GREAT THAT HAPPENED TODAY

_____

_____

_____

 THIS PERSON BROUGHT ME JOY TODAY

_____

_____

DATE: S M T W TH F S ___ / ___ / ___

ONLY POSITIVE THOUGHTS IN MY DAY
I can make today awesome by:

_____

_____

_____

DRAW IT!

what are you
looking forward
to most today?

I LOVE MYSELF
LIST 3 THINGS YOU HOPE TO DO THIS WEEK

TODAY I SMILED BECAUSE

_____

_____

_____

TODAY I FELT

SOMETHING GREAT THAT HAPPENED TODAY

_____

_____

_____

 THIS PERSON BROUGHT ME JOY TODAY

_____

_____

DATE: S M T W TH F S ___/___/___

ONLY POSITIVE THOUGHTS IN MY DAY
I can make today awesome by:

_____

_____

_____

DRAW IT!

what are you looking forward to most today?

I LOVE MYSELF
LIST 3 THINGS YOU LOOK FORWARD TO

WHEN I FEEL MAD THIS IS WHAT I DO

_____

_____

_____

TODAY I FELT

SOMETHING GREAT THAT HAPPENED TODAY

_____

_____

_____

 THIS PERSON BROUGHT ME JOY TODAY

_____

_____

DATE: S M T W TH F S ___/___/___

ONLY POSITIVE THOUGHTS IN MY DAY
I can make today awesome by:

_____

_____

_____

DRAW IT!

what are you looking forward to most today?

I LOVE MYSELF
LIST 3 THINGS YOU DID THAT YOU WERE PROUD OF DOING

I'M GRATEFUL FOR

_____

_____

_____

TODAY I FELT

SOMETHING GREAT THAT HAPPENED TODAY

_____

_____

_____

 THIS PERSON BROUGHT ME JOY TODAY

_____

_____

DATE: **S M T W TH F S** ___/___/___

ONLY POSITIVE THOUGHTS IN MY DAY
I can make today awesome by:

_____

_____

_____

DRAW IT!

what are you looking forward to most today?

I LOVE MYSELF
LIST 3 THINGS YOU ARE EXCITED ABOUT

WHAT I'M LOVING ABOUT LIFE RIGHT NOW

_____

_____

_____

TODAY I FELT

SOMETHING GREAT THAT HAPPENED TODAY

_____

_____

_____

 ## THIS PERSON BROUGHT ME JOY TODAY

_____

_____

DATE: S M T W TH F S ___/___/___

ONLY POSITIVE THOUGHTS IN MY DAY
I can make today awesome by:

_____

_____

_____

DRAW IT!
what are you looking forward to most today?

I LOVE MYSELF
LIST 3 THINGS YOU ARE THANKFUL FOR

MY FAVORITE PERSON TO BE AROUND IS

_____

_____

_____

TODAY I FELT

SOMETHING GREAT THAT HAPPENED TODAY

_____

_____

_____

 ## THIS PERSON BROUGHT ME JOY TODAY

_____

_____

DATE: **S M T W TH F S**   ___/___/___

ONLY POSITIVE THOUGHTS IN MY DAY
I can make today awesome by:

_____

_____

_____

DRAW IT!

what are you
looking forward
to most today?

I LOVE MYSELF
LIST 3 WAYS YOUR LIFE IS AWESOME

THE PERSON I MOST ADMIRE IS

_____

_____

_____

TODAY I FELT

SOMETHING GREAT THAT HAPPENED TODAY

_____

_____

_____

THIS PERSON BROUGHT ME JOY TODAY

_____

_____

DATE: S M T W TH F S ___/___/___

ONLY POSITIVE THOUGHTS IN MY DAY
I can make today awesome by:

_____

_____

_____

DRAW IT!
what are you
looking forward
to most today?

I LOVE MYSELF
LIST 3 THINGS YOU DID THIS WEEK

THIS IS WHAT BRINGS ME HAPPINESS

_____

_____

_____

TODAY I FELT

SOMETHING GREAT THAT HAPPENED TODAY

_____

_____

_____

 THIS PERSON BROUGHT ME JOY TODAY

_____

_____

DATE: S M T W TH F S ___/___/___

ONLY POSITIVE THOUGHTS IN MY DAY

I can make today awesome by:

_____

_____

_____

DRAW IT!

what are you looking forward to most today?

I LOVE MYSELF

LIST 3 SMALL SUCCESS YOU HAD THIS WEEK

THIS ALWAYS MAKES ME SMILE

_____

_____

_____

TODAY I FELT

SOMETHING GREAT THAT HAPPENED TODAY

_____

_____

_____

 THIS PERSON BROUGHT ME JOY TODAY

_____

_____

DATE: S M T W TH F S ___/___/___

ONLY POSITIVE THOUGHTS IN MY DAY

I can make today awesome by:

_____

_____

_____

DRAW IT!

what are you looking forward to most today?

I LOVE MYSELF

LIST 3 THINGS YOU LIKE ABOUT YOURSELF

MY FAVORITE PART OF TODAY

_____

_____

_____

TODAY I FELT

SOMETHING GREAT THAT HAPPENED TODAY

_____

_____

_____

 ## THIS PERSON BROUGHT ME JOY TODAY

_____

_____

DATE: S M T W TH F S ___/___/___

ONLY POSITIVE THOUGHTS IN MY DAY
I can make today awesome by:

_____

_____

_____

DRAW IT!

what are you
looking forward
to most today?

I LOVE MYSELF
LIST 3 WORDS THAT DESCRIBE YOU

WHAT I'M LOOKING FORWARD TO TOMORROW

_____

_____

_____

TODAY I FELT

SOMETHING GREAT THAT HAPPENED TODAY

_____

_____

_____

THIS PERSON BROUGHT ME JOY TODAY

_____

_____

Made in the USA
Coppell, TX
03 September 2021

61749779R00063